To Mom + Dad

A combined Birthday
Present on a great day.

June 1993

Scott + Jan + Melissa

MULLIGAN'S LAWS

ALSO BY HENRY BEARD

THE OFFICIAL EXCEPTIONS TO THE RULES OF GOLF

FRENCH FOR CATS

ADVANCED FRENCH FOR EXCEPTIONAL CATS

LATIN FOR ALL OCCASIONS

LATIN FOR EVEN MORE OCCASIONS

MISS PIGGY'S GUIDE TO LIFE

SAILING: A SAILOR'S DICTIONARY

FISHING: AN ANGLER'S DICTIONARY

GOLFING: A DUFFER'S DICTIONARY

SKIING: A SKIER'S DICTIONARY

MULLIGAN'S LAWS

BY THOMAS MULLIGAN, FOURTH EARL OF MURPHY

A Lifetime of Golfing Wisdom from the
Genius Who Invented the Do-Over

EDITED BY

Henry Beard

SKETCHES RESTORED BY
WILLIAM RUGGIERI

A JOHN BOSWELL ASSOCIATES BOOK

DOUBLEDAY
NEW YORK LONDON TORONTO SYDNEY AUCKLAND

PUBLISHED BY DOUBLEDAY
a division of Bantam Doubleday Dell Publishing Group, Inc.
1540 Broadway, New York, New York 10036

DOUBLEDAY and the portrayal of an anchor with a dolphin are
trademarks of Doubleday, a division of Bantam Doubleday Dell
Publishing Group, Inc.

Library of Congress Cataloging-in-Publication Data
Beard, Henry
       Mulligan's laws : a lifetime of golfing wisdom from the
       genious who invented the do-over by Thomas Mulligan, fourth
       earl of Murphy/edited by Henry Beard.—1st ed.
          p.   cm.
        ISBN 0-385-46999-3
        1.Golf—Humor. I. Title
        GV967.M39 1993   93-9242
        796.352 ' 0207—dc20   CIP

CONTENTS

INTRODUCTION • VII

THE GAME • 1

THE PLAYER • 17

THE MATCH • 33

THE COURSE • 49

THE CLUBS • 65

THE BALL • 81

THE CLUBHOUSE • 97

THE MYSTERY OF MULLIGAN

Everywhere in the world, whenever golfers hit a miserable drive on the first hole, and then quickly tee up a second ball for a do-over, they invariably invoke the most famous name in the history of the game—Mulligan.

And yet, until now, absolutely nothing has been known about the legendary hacker who conceived the single most crucial and sensible modification of the Rules of Golf ever devised. In fact, some misguided students of the game have even made the farfetched suggestion that there was no actual Mulligan, and that the term is nothing more than a contraction of the phrase "maul it again."

But if Mulligan really did exist, as surely he must have, then who was he, and how could the remarkable man who discovered the golfing equivalent of penicillin in what had to have been comparatively recent times been so swiftly and thoroughly forgotten?

Our dramatic discovery of the answers to these questions came about entirely by accident. Following the publication in the spring of 1992 of *The Official Exceptions to the Rules of Golf* and its subsequent international success, we were contacted by a private collector of golf memorabilia who told us that the subversive and antiestablishment tone of the book had convinced him to share with us what he described as "golf's greatest treasure—the Mulligan archives." His only condition was absolute confidentiality.

We soon had reason to understand both the basis for his enthusiasm and the grounds for his caution.

In the seclusion of his private library in his comfortable country house in a town in Ireland we are not at liberty to name, this gentleman removed from a battered leather briefcase a little plaid-covered book—the very book that, in a slightly modernized typeset version,* you now hold in your hands.

When we opened this slim volume and saw the name of Thomas Mulligan on the title page, we experienced the kind of thrill biblical scholars must have felt when the Dead Sea Scrolls were unrolled for the first time. As we perused the handwritten pages filled with Mulligan's amazing insights into golf and those who play it and his ingenious sketches of ideas for innovations in the

---

*Readers will from time to time come upon references in the text to present-day golfers like Corey Pavin and John Daly and equipment, such as a 7-iron or a wedge, that didn't exist in Mulligan's time (except in his fertile imagination). These apparent anachronisms are simply contemporary equivalents that we have substituted for dated names and terms, like "Old Tom Morris" and "mashie-niblick," in the interest of making Mulligan's work more accessible to a modern audience. We have, of course, made every effort to retain his original meaning.

game that would not be introduced for many decades to come, we realized with growing excitement that we were looking at the work of a man who was both the Plato and the da Vinci of golf.

The briefcase also contained a birth certificate and a handful of other legal documents, an album of daguerreotype photographs of Mulligan (one of which is reproduced on the cover), a few letters, enough material for a sequel, and a single scorecard with an 89 entered on it from the Ballydormie golf links in Kilroy, which, as near as can be told from the small location map printed on one side of the card, now lie under one of the runways at Shannon airport.

The few pieces of biographical data that we were able to assemble from these various 19th-century artifacts indicate that Mulligan was a minor Anglo-Irish aristocrat and passionate golfer who was born on May 1, 1793, and who lived near Lough Sclaff, on the Shannon estuary, in a modest manor house called Duffnaught Hall, which was totally destroyed in a mysterious fire one week after his death on April 1, 1879.

When we inquired of our reclusive collector why no one knew even these meager details of Mulligan's life, his answer was as chilling as it was plausible.

Mulligan, he explained, was the target of a far-reaching and very nearly successful campaign on the part of the Golf Establishment which, within a week of his funeral, sent squads of goons to eradicate from the face of the earth any and all traces of the heretic who had dared to humanize the rigid and cold hearted game they ruled with an iron grip.

That his extraordinary manuscript managed to survive this sinister conspiracy by the game's shadowy ruling elite is apparently a matter of pure luck. By the time of his death, Mulligan had crammed his locker at his home course so full of clubs, spare clothing, and other odds and ends that he simply couldn't wedge another thing in, even something as small as a notebook, and thus his great masterpiece was spared incineration in the suspicious explosion that leveled the old clubhouse on April 8, 1879.

There isn't room here to tell the story of how Mulligan's caddie used a lifetime of match play cunning to preserve his master's literary legacy from the clutches of the R & A's thugs, or, for that matter, to recount the dozens of baffling mishaps that have plagued this project since we first obtained Mulligan's long-lost manuscript—the puzzling grounding of the *QE2* on which one of the duplicate copies was shipped and from which it vanished, the unexplained burglaries of our offices, the odd boiler accident at the printing plant. Suffice it to say that to this day, the guardians of golfing orthodoxy have not abandoned their efforts to suppress the works of this veritable Martin Luther of the links.

We are truly honored to have played a part, however small, in bringing Mulligan's magnum opus to the millions of his fellow hackers for whom it was originally written well over a century ago, and we feel that it is indeed fitting that *Mulligan's Laws* is being published on the 200th anniversary of his birth.

With this happy coincidence in mind, we think it is appropriate to suggest that, as a demonstration of respect to the man who tamed the first tee, golfers everywhere honor his memory on May 1, 1993, and on the first Saturday in May in subsequent years, by taking a mulligan on the tee of every hole they play that day.

Pick up that putt, too.

"Inasmuch as strokes taken after play is concluded on the 18th hole do not count towards the total entered on one's tally card, it seems to me eminently reasonable that any shots struck before play is properly commenced with a satisfactory drive on the first tee should be of no more consequence to one's score than those swings which one has made by way of practice in the course of hitting balls upon the driving ground."

Thomas Mulligan, Fourth Earl of Murphy
Diary entry dated 7 June 1845

THE GAME

"I for one would be most pleased to dispense with the company of the various and sundry morons, felons, and malcontents employed at the links as caddies were I not loath to be a pack animal for my own sack of clubs. A mechanical golf carriage would seem an admirable substitute for these sullen louts, and whatever noises might be produced by its engine would be far preferable to the grunts and snickers of some gin-stunned nincompoop."—*MULLIGAN'S DIARY*

The game of golf is 90% mental and 10% mental

Error must go somewhere*

***If your driver is hot, your putter will be ice-cold; if
you can hit your irons, you will top your woods; if
you are keeping your right elbow tucked in, your
head will come up**

● ●

It's as easy to lower your handicap as it is to reduce your hat size

•

If you really want to get better at golf, go back and take it up at a much earlier age

The secret of golf is, use your real swing to take the
big divot, use your practice swing to make the shot,
and always hit the do-over first

•

The only thing you can learn from golf books is that
you can't learn anything from golf books, but you
have to read an awful lot of golf books to learn it

The stages of a golfer's game are: Sudden Collapse, Radical Change, Complete Frustration, Slow Improvement, Brief Mastery, and Sudden Collapse

•

Progress in golf consists of two steps forward, and 26.6 miles backward

•

If you can keep your head when the wheels come off your game, you need a new head

Strokes always accumulate faster than they can be forgotten

●

Since bad shots come in groups of three, a fourth bad shot is actually the beginning of the next group of three

●

One good shank deserves another

When you look up and cause an awful shot, you will always look down again at exactly the moment when you ought to start watching the ball if you ever want to see it again

•

If the wind is in your face, you swing too hard just to get the ball through it; if the wind is at your back, you swing too hard just to see how far you can get the ball to go

The one drive you really nail will always be hit on a
hole with no carry

•

Whenever you play in a mixed foursome, there will
always be at least one hole where you have to hit your
second shot before the ladies tee off

The only sure way to find a drive sliced deep into the woods is to hit a provisional ball 260 yards down the middle

•

The only sure way to hit a perfectly straight 260-yard drive is to decide not to go for it on a dogleg hole

•

The only sure way to get a par is to leave a four-foot birdie putt two inches short of the hole

The odds of making a hole are 1 in 30,000 unless:

1. You are playing alone, in which case they are 1 in 1,000

2. You are playing alone and even with the ace, you still have no chance of breaking 90, in which case they are 1 in 100

3. You are playing alone, you cannot break 90, and either you sneaked onto the course or called in sick in order to play, in which case they are 1 in 10

It takes 17 holes to really get warmed up

•

If you know you're going to have to quit before the end of a round, you'll par all the remaining holes

•

You can hear thunder a hundred miles away when you're three holes down with three to play

No golfer ever swung too slowly

•

No golfer ever played too fast

•

No golfer ever dressed too plainly

One birdie is a hot streak

•

The putt breaks the other way

•

It's always the caddie's fault

THE PLAYER

"Anyone who has observed the tenacity with which a thistle will attach itself to a wool jacket when one has been obliged to play a shot from the gorse cannot fail to see therein the essence of a new method of fastening every sort of strap or belt. I can think of no better use for this discovery than on the back of a glove, which one is forever fumbling to remove before putting. The distracting noise made when the thistle backing is torn from the woolen lining is merely an additional benefit."—MULLIGAN'S DIARY

Don't play with anyone who would question a 7

No matter how badly you are playing, it is always possible to play worse

•

Whatever you think you're doing wrong is the one thing you're doing right

•

Any change works for three holes

$$D = nP^2 \text{ *}$$

*The odds of hitting a duffed shot increase by the square of the number of people watching

Never take lessons from your father

•

Never teach golf to your wife

•

Never play your son for money

The more memorable the swing thought, the more useless the information it conveys

•

Never try to keep more than 300 separate thoughts in your mind during your swing

The three keys to playing golf well:

1. Keep your head still

2. Keep your stupid head still

3. Keep your goddam stupid head still

When your shot has to carry over a water hazard, you can either hit one more club or two more balls

•

If you're afraid a full shot might reach the green while the foursome ahead is still putting out, you have two options: You can immediately shank a lay-up, or you can wait until the green is clear and top a ball halfway there

The less skilled the player, the more likely he is to share his ideas about the golf swing

•

The less intelligent the player, the more certain he is to offer insights into the mental side of the game

Mulligan's Etiquette

1. Always replace divots in the fairway and rake footprints in the sand trap even if you have to move your ball to do so

2. Always give faster players some reason, no matter how lame, for why you won't let them play through

3. Never use another player's ball on the same hole where you stole it

4. Don't cut in on a hole if both the tee and green are occupied and there is someone in the fairway

5. Remember that it only takes a few extra seconds to pick up a wedge left on the green by a group of slower players in front of you and throw it deep into the woods

The inevitable result of any golf lesson is the instant
elimination of the one critical unconscious motion
that allowed you to compensate for all your errors

●

The source of your latest swing fault is a recent
correction

●

If it ain't broke, try changing your grip

There are no little problems

•

There are no tiny changes

•

There are no small pieces of advice

Everyone replaces his divot after a perfect
approach shot

•

There are no atheists in pot bunkers

•

Golfers who claim they never cheat also lie

Slow players are early risers

•

When another foursome is on the green, "Fore!" is
not an excuse, "So what?" is not an apology, and
"Up yours" is not an explanation

•

Nice guys finish in the dark

THE MATCH

"*After much study of the matter, I have concluded that the fairest method of determining when a short putt should be conceded is to imagine that a putter is laid upon the green with its head alongside the hole and its shaft beside the ball, and if the ball then be no further from the hole than the end of the leather of the grip, a player may pick it up, but he should be quick about it, and if he be such an imbecile as to choose to putt it, even for practice, and he misses, he forfeits the 'Give Ye.'*"—MULLIGAN'S DIARY

There is no such thing as a friendly wager

A golf match is a test of your skill against your
opponent's luck

•

The lower the stakes in any match, the more
outrageous the behavior of its participants

•

Good sportsmanship is as essential to the game of
golf as good penmanship is to stock car racing

$$P^t = \pi \, P^g \text{ *}$$

*The length of a putt you are entitled to take is exactly 3.14 times the length of a putt you are willing to give

In any best-ball match, the smaller the significance
of your partner's putt, the greater the probability
that he will sink it

•

Taking more than two putts to get down on a
lightning-fast, steeply sloped green is no
embarrassment unless you had to hit a wedge
between the putts

•

It's surprisingly easy to hole a 50-foot putt when
you lie 10

Never leave your opponent with the sole
responsibility for thinking of all the things that might
go wrong with his shot

•

Counting on your opponent to inform you when he
breaks a rule is like expecting him to make fun of his
own haircut

•

If your opponent hasn't played the course before,
don't be a spoilsport and ruin all the surprises

The score a player reports on any hole should
always be regarded as his opening offer

•

Never subtract so many strokes on any one hole
that you wind up with the honor on the next tee

•

The statute of limitations on forgotten strokes is
two holes

Mulligan's Principles of Golf Chemistry

1. Bets lengthen putts and shorten drives

2. Confidence evaporates in the presence of water

3. In the heat of a match, balls tend to rise to the surface of the rough

4. It takes considerable pressure to make a penalty stroke adhere to a scorecard

5. No matter how much energy you expend, it's impossible to lower the stakes or raise your handicap

6. Over time, any putter can reach a temperature of absolute zero

7. If the loss is sufficiently infuriating, matter can be destroyed

Nonchalant putts count the same as chalant putts

•

It's not a gimme if you're still away

•

A tap-in is the larval stage of a hop-out

In any match, the odds against playing another hole well double after each successive well-played hole*

*The odds against playing all 18 holes well are $2^{18} : 1$

Tennis would be as difficult as golf if you only got one
serve, six-love, six-love were par, you often lost a
dozen balls in a single set, and every now and then
you had to hit a backhand out of a tree

The more often your opponent quotes the rules, the greater the certainty that he cheats

•

The more your opponent stresses the importance of etiquette, the better the odds that he will sneeze in your backswing

The only time you play great golf is when you are
doing everything within your power to lose to your
boss

•

Whenever there is money riding on a hole, someone
will appear riding on a mower

Don't call your shots

•

Never putt a gimme

•

Always limp with the same leg for the whole round

THE COURSE

"Where due to lack of adequate room or the absence of sufficient funds it is not practical to construct a golf course, an opportunity to play may still be afforded to the populace by constructing a sort of Lilliputian links where the putter is the only club employed, and the twists and turns of ingeniously sited ramps and chutes, and their interruption by fanciful obstacles, provide the sport. NOTE: To prevent the ball being purloined, a sort of drain-pipe could be affixed to the underside of the 18th hole."—MULLIGAN'S DIARY

The rake is in the other trap

The wind is in your face on 16 of the 18 holes

•

Play is faster on the other nine

•

You always have the honor on a tricky par three

The shortest distance between any two points on a golf course is a straight line that passes directly through the center of a very large tree

•

Nothing straightens out a nasty slice quicker than a sharp dogleg to the right

It's often necessary to hit a second drive to really appreciate the first one

•

The worse your drive is stymied, the more perfectly it would have played on the previous hole

The tees are always back

•

The rough will be mown tomorrow

•

The ball always lands where the pin was yesterday

$$C = {}^D\!/_{10}*$$

*You need to bring one extra club for every 10 yards between your ball and the closest point to it that you can drive the cart

Electric carts never die at the turn

•

It never begins to rain when you're on the 18th hole

•

It always takes at least five holes to notice that a club is missing

On courses where the yardages are marked on
sprinkler heads:

1. There will be no sprinkler head within 40 yards
of your ball

2. The nearest sprinkler head will be blank

3. While being examined, the sprinkler head will
turn on

There are two kinds of bounces: unfair bounces, and bounces just the way you meant to play it

•

Never claim that you really intended to skip the ball across the water, or stop it against a rake handle, or bang it off the top of the flagstick

Mulligan's Quantum Theory of the Golf Links

1. A stroke does not occur unless it is observed by more than one golfer

2. 99.99% of all matter is empty space, but that last .01% will stop a golf ball dead

3. If your ball disappears in the fairway of a blind hole, it's probably because it rolled into an antidivot and vaporized

4. Time can run backwards if there are women on the course

5. If the moon had an evenly dimpled surface and a rubber core, a couple of Out of Bounds stakes could pull it out of its orbit

6. Every time a golfer makes a birdie, he must subsequently make two triple bogeys to restore the fundamental equilibrium of the universe

The most difficult lie in golf is a ball sitting up in the dead center of the fairway 150 yards from the pin

•

You can hit a 2-acre fairway 10% of the time, and a 2-inch branch 90% of the time

•

No matter how short the par three, the drive is never a gimme

Out of Bounds is always on the right

•

Two thirds of the holes are uphill

•

The practice putting green is either half as fast or
twice as fast as all the other greens

If you're the only one who improves his lie, it's cheating; if you all improve your lies, it's a perfectly reasonable adjustment of obviously unfair playing conditions

•

There's no ground that couldn't use a little repair

•

It's always winter somewhere

THE CLUBS

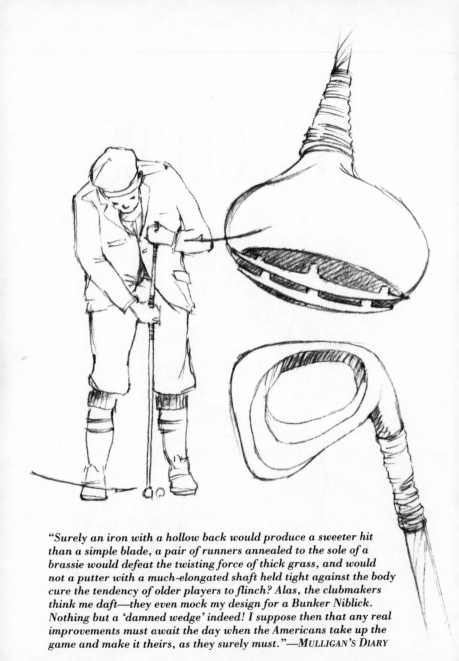

"Surely an iron with a hollow back would produce a sweeter hit than a simple blade, a pair of runners annealed to the sole of a brassie would defeat the twisting force of thick grass, and would not a putter with a much-elongated shaft held tight against the body cure the tendency of older players to flinch? Alas, the clubmakers think me daft—they even mock my design for a Bunker Niblick. Nothing but a 'damned wedge' indeed! I suppose then that any real improvements must await the day when the Americans take up the game and make it theirs, as they surely must."—MULLIGAN'S DIARY

No one with funny headcovers ever broke par

If swinging the club really was as simple and natural
as, say, swinging a hammer, Corey Pavin would be
making $8.47 an hour

•

If it really made sense to "let the club do the work,"
you'd just say, "Driver, wedge to the green, one-
putt," and walk to the next tee

Your straightest iron shot of the day will be exactly one club short

•

If you want to hit a 7-iron as far as John Daly does, simply play to lay up just short of a water hazard

The lowest numbered iron in your bag will always be
impossible to hit*

*If you leave your 2-iron at home, then your 3-iron
will become impossible to hit; if you leave your 2- and
your 3-irons at home, your 4-iron will become
impossible to hit

When you select a club for a shot to the green, there are three possible outcomes:

1. It's the right club, but you change your mind

2. It's the right club, but in the middle of your backswing you decide it's the wrong club, so you hit it too hard or too easy

3. It's the wrong club

$$S_d = S_b H^*$$

*To calculate the speed of a player's downswing,
multiply the speed of his backswing by his handicap.
Example: backswing 40 mph, handicap 15,
downswing 600 mph

There is no movement in the golf swing so difficult
that it cannot be made even more difficult by careful
study and diligent practice

•

Any swing drill or shotmaking tip that you just
couldn't get the hang of during a one-hour lesson will
be immediately mastered by the first player you
describe it to

Whatever you leave out of your bag is the one thing you will need*

*If it is Band-Aids, you will develop a blister; if it is rain gear, it will pour; if it is a spare glove, yours will tear on the fifth hole

The number of tees in your bag is always less than 3 or more than 600

•

No matter how far its shaft extends, a ball retriever is always a foot too short to reach the ball

Knowing the swingweight of your club is as
indispensable to playing good golf as knowing the
temperature of the grass in the fairway

•

There are two things you can learn by stopping your
backswing at the top and checking the position of your
hands: how many hands you have, and which one is
wearing the glove

If you seem to be hitting your shots straight on the driving range, it's probably because you're not aiming at anything

•

The only thing of real value that you can take from the driving range to the first tee is a pocketful of range balls

Few golfers are born with a natural talent for hitting the ball, but every player is blessed with the God-given ability to throw a club

•

All of the basic movements of a perfectly executed pivot can be easily duplicated by using a forceful turning motion of your body to toss a bag full of clubs into a pond

A two-foot putt counts the same as a two-foot drive

•

You can hit the ball 75 yards with any club in the bag

•

You really only need four clubs to hit every bad shot in golf

THE BALL

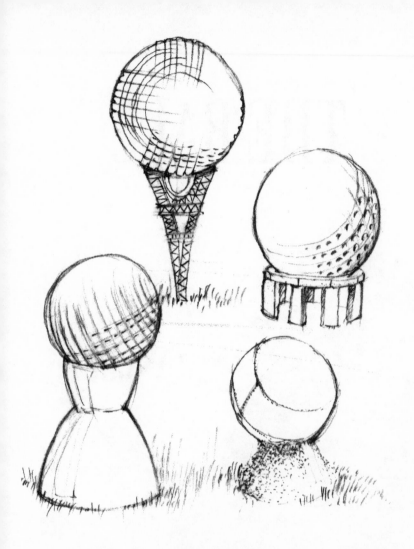

"Perching the ball upon a dollop of moist sand to elevate it for the drive is a most difficult method of accomplishing this objective. It must be possible to fashion some sort of prong on which to place it, though I would concede that if such an appliance existed, one would doubtless run out of the things on the 7th hole. On the other hand, a packet of these Tee Nails, perhaps imprinted with a player's name, would make an ideal birthday gift."—*MULLIGAN'S DIARY*

Hazards attract; fairways repel

•

No animal will ever steal your ball from a bunker

Never wash your ball on the tee of a water hole

It's a simple matter to keep your ball in the fairway if you're not too choosy about which fairway

●

The harder you try to keep your ball from landing in a particular place, the more certain it is that it will go there

●

You can put your ball in even the smallest fairway bunker if you aim at it

A ball will always come to rest halfway down a hill
unless there is sand or water at the bottom

•

A ball will always seek the lowest possible point in
which to lie so long as that point is not a perfectly
round hole 4½ inches in diameter and 4 inches deep

A ball hit to the wrong green will always land two feet from the hole

•

The only time your ball ever bites is when it lands 30 feet short

•

A practice ball hit from a bunker in disgust after a flubbed explosion shot will always stop right next to the pin

For most golfers, the only difference between a
one-dollar ball and a three-dollar ball is two dollars

•

You can put "draw" on the ball, you can put "fade"
on the ball, but no golfer can put "straight" on the
ball

A ball hit into the rough will always disappear
between two identical shrubs

•

If you can't find your ball in the rough, but you do
find another ball nearby that you could easily play, it
will be orange, yellow, or pink

•

A ball you searched for for five minutes will be found
in five seconds by a player in the first foursome
behind you

The Four Forces of Golf Ball Physics

1. *Gravity*, which causes the ball to drop suddenly into hazards and deep rough

2. *Electromagnetism*, which makes it curve sharply towards whichever of the earth's poles is closest to the right side of the fairway

3. *The Weak Force*, which makes it dribble to the edge of the ladies' tee

4. *The Strong Force*, which propels it directly towards a foursome of lawyers in the next fairway

$$F = (f) S^{*}$$

*The frequency with which balls are lost increases as the available supply decreases

Mulligan's Laws of Motion

1. No matter how precarious or unstable its lie, a ball at rest will tend to remain at rest until the moment it is addressed

2. A ball will always travel farthest when hit in the wrong direction

3. Every distortion in the flight of the ball towards its target produces an equal and opposite contortion in the body of the player who hit it

No putt ever got longer as the result of a ball being
marked

•

Spike marks in the path of an off-line putt will never
deflect the ball into the hole

A ball you can see in the rough from 50 yards away
is not yours

•

If there is a ball in the fringe and a ball in the bunker,
your ball is in the bunker

•

If both balls are in the bunker, yours is in the footprint

You can lead a horse to water, but you can't make it retrieve your ball

•

An extra ball in the pocket is worth two strokes in the bush

•

A penny saved is an excellent ball marker

THE
CLUBHOUSE

kippers

stilton cheese

cucumbers

toothpick

toast

tomato

chicken

toast

bacon

lettuce

toast

"This compact repast is designed for simplicity of preparation and swiftness of consumption in the Clubhouse in the midst of a round. It could be accompanied by potatoes fried in the French fashion and a glass of chilled tea or a bottle of lager, and in that regard, I do wish that some method might be devised to brew a beer of a lighter character that would tend less to fill one up and yet retain superior taste."—MULLIGAN'S DIARY

Nature abhors a half-empty locker

There's always a doctor on the one pay phone

•

You can't get to the bathroom without taking off
your spikes

•

There are nicer towels on the ballwashers

All they have is cream soda, diet Fanta, and cherry Gatorade

•

You always have the feeling you've already read the latest issue of any golf magazine

•

The guy in the next locker cracks his knuckles, smells like a bus, and knows 1100 golf jokes

The more exclusive the club, the greater the risk of
food poisoning

•

Unless you're already bald, don't use the comb in the
jar of blue fluid

If the course is completely empty when you drive up, it's because an outing of 100 golfers is getting ready to tee off in a shotgun start

•

If you aren't paired with the two jerks you saw unloading their clubs in the parking lot, it's because there's a couple from hell waiting for you on the putting green

No matter how early your tee time, there will always
be a foursome in the middle of the first fairway

•

If you ever par the first three holes, you'll have a
20-minute wait on the fourth tee

•

The only really useful golf tip is one given to the
starter to get you out ahead of a mixed foursome

Never ask the pro if you need a new set of clubs

•

Don't buy a putter until you've had a chance
to throw it

The Pro Shop Laws of Supply and Demand

1. They have extra spikes, but they don't fit your shoes

2. They have the kind of glove you like, but not your size

3. All the hats are yellow

4. A bag of tees costs $4.00

5. The rental set has Sunbeam irons, Tommy Bolt woods, and a Black & Decker putter

6. The only cheap balls are Proctor-Silex X-outs

The inappropriateness of attire worn by prospective players at a private or resort course increases in direct proportion to the accumulation of unsold inventory in its pro shop

•

If you are unsure whether your clothing is suitable for wear on a golf course, ask yourself if it combines the minimum imaginable taste with the maximum possible discomfort

The best way to cause the prompt reappearance of a
club lost on the course is to order a replacement

●

The best way to tell whether any golf gadget will help
your game is to try to picture Freddie Couples using
one

● ●

The people who buy houses on golf courses always
seem surprised to discover that a game in which balls
are hit with considerable force is being played
practically in their backyards

•

The people on the greenkeeping staff always look
like they took the job because a golf course is such a
terrific place to dispose of all the bodies

If you stop for lunch between nines, you will
overhear a conversation featuring the words "choke"
and "shank"

•

If you stop for a beer at the end of the round, you
will hear someone bitching about a 78

Four days of perfect weather begin on Monday

ABOUT THE EDITOR

●

Henry Beard was a founder of the *National Lampoon* and was its editor during the heyday of the magazine in the 1970s. He is the author of a number of best-selling humorous books, including *Miss Piggy's Guide to Life*, *French for Cats*, *Latin for All Occasions*, and, with Christopher Cerf, *The Official Politically Correct Dictionary and Handbook*. He also wrote the two golf classics *Golfing: A Duffer's Dictionary* and *The Official Exceptions to the Rules of Golf*. A 14-handicap player, he recently shot his own weight at Pebble Beach.